TinkerActive

EARLY SKILLS · WORKBOOKS

Ages 3+

English
Language Arts

written by **Kate Avino**

educational consulting by **Casey Federico, MSEd**

illustrated by **Gustavo Almeida**

odd dot

NEW YORK

120 Broadway
New York, NY 10271
OddDot.com

ISBN: 978-1-250-78441-4

WRITER Kate Avino

ILLUSTRATOR Gustavo Almeida

EDUCATIONAL CONSULTANT Casey Federico, MSEd

CHARACTER DESIGNER Anna-Maria Jung

DESIGNER Tim Hall

EDITOR Nathalie Le Du and Peter Mavrikis

Our books may be purchased in bulk for promotional, educational, or business use. Please contact your local bookseller or the Macmillan Corporate and Premium Sales Department at (800) 221-7945 ext. 5442 or by email at MacmillanSpecialMarkets@macmillan.com.

Printed in China by Hung Hing Off-set Printing Co. Ltd.,
Heshan City, Guangdong Province

First edition, 2023

1 3 5 7 9 10 8 6 4 2

Meet the MotMots!

 Amelia
 Brian
 Callie
 Dimitri
 Enid
 Frank

Drawing Uppercase Letter Shapes

Welcome to Tinker Town's farm! Draw lines to complete the barn. Start at each ▶ and end at each ⬤.

★ HEY, GROWN-UPS! ★

Drawing vertical and horizontal lines helps children write letters later on in this book. Don't worry if your child's lines aren't straight or if they veer off the path.

Draw a line from each MotMot to their .

Good job! You earned a sticker! Choose one from page 127 and place it on your poster. When you see this corner, choose a new sticker!

2

Draw a line from each  to its .

Draw a line from each to its _____ .

The chickens are on the loose!
Draw a line from each  to its .

★ HEY, GROWN-UPS! ★

Your child's hands are getting stronger, and they will soon be able to tightly grip a pencil. Encourage your child to strengthen their hands and fingers by playing with clay, crayons, or rubber bands, or by helping you stir while cooking!

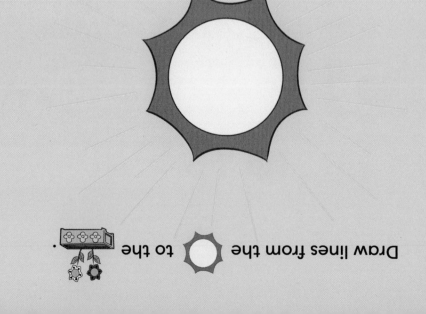

Draw lines from the to the .

Draw lines to complete the pens.

Draw a line from each MotMot to their .

Draw a line from each animal to its home.

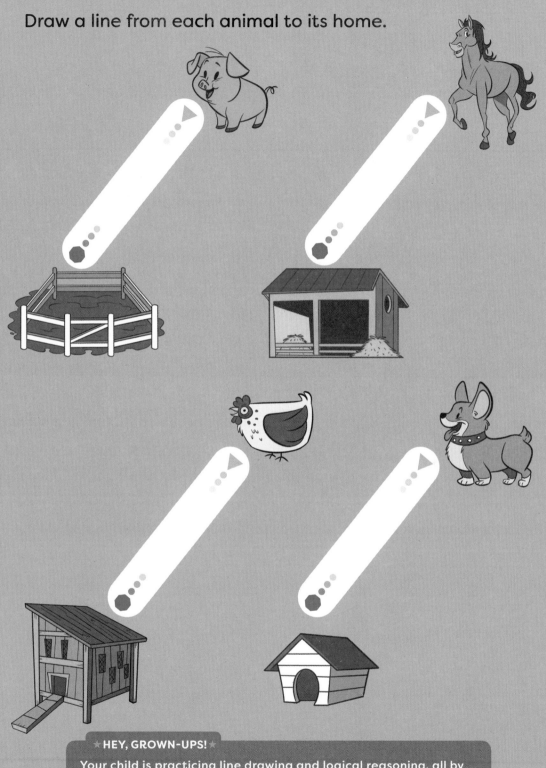

Draw a line from each to its .

Dimitri is giving the barn dogs a bath!
Draw lines around the bubbles.

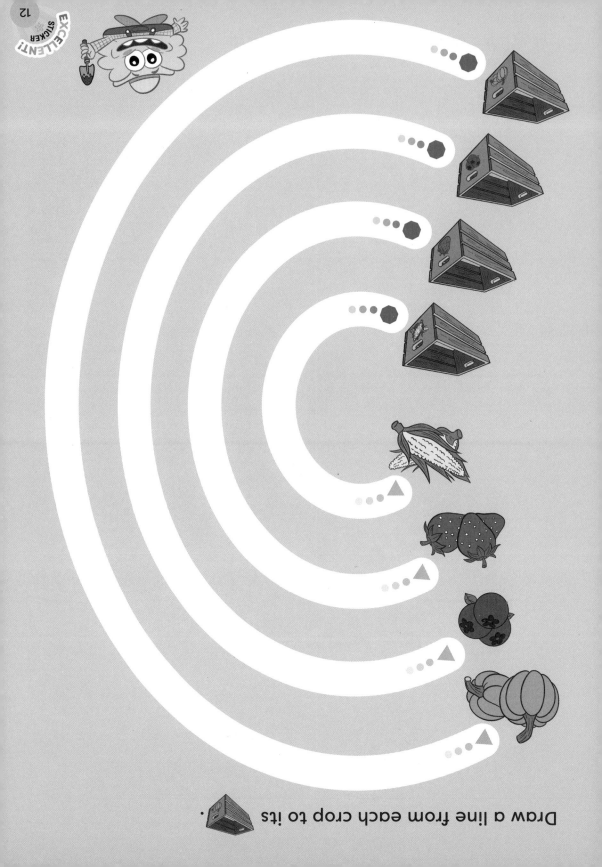

Draw a line from each crop to its

Let's TINKER!

Gather these tools and materials.

Play with your materials. How can you tell which materials are straight and which are curved? Can you bend any of the straight materials so they become curved?

Ink pad or washable paint

Marker or crayon

White paper

Craft sticks or paper straws

Giant marshmallows

Let's MAKE!

Connecting-Dot Art!

1. **Press** a finger or thumb into the ink pad or washable paint.

2. Make dots all over the paper.

3. Draw lines to connect the dots.

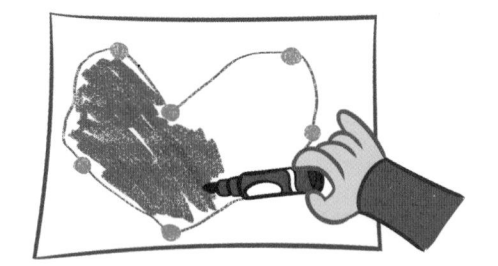

4. Color in or decorate your shapes.

Let's ENGINEER a solution!

The animals broke through their pen! How can Amelia and Brian keep the animals in the yard? **Pretend** your connecting-dot art is the farm's yard. **Build** a gate around it using your materials. Can you make a straight fence? What about a curved fence?

You're a TinkerActive CHAMPION!

You've earned an extra-special sticker. Peel it and place it anywhere you'd like on your poster.

Tracing Uppercase Letter Shapes

It's harvest time! Trace the dotted line from each MotMot to their crop.

★ HEY, GROWN-UPS! ★

In the last chapter, your child drew lines within a wide path. Now your child will draw directly on a dotted line. Tracing dotted lines is a new and more challenging skill for your little learner. If they veer off the line, don't worry! You can draw more dotted lines on the write-and-wipe game board and ask your child to trace them for extra practice.

Trace the line from each 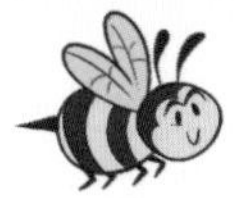 to its plant.

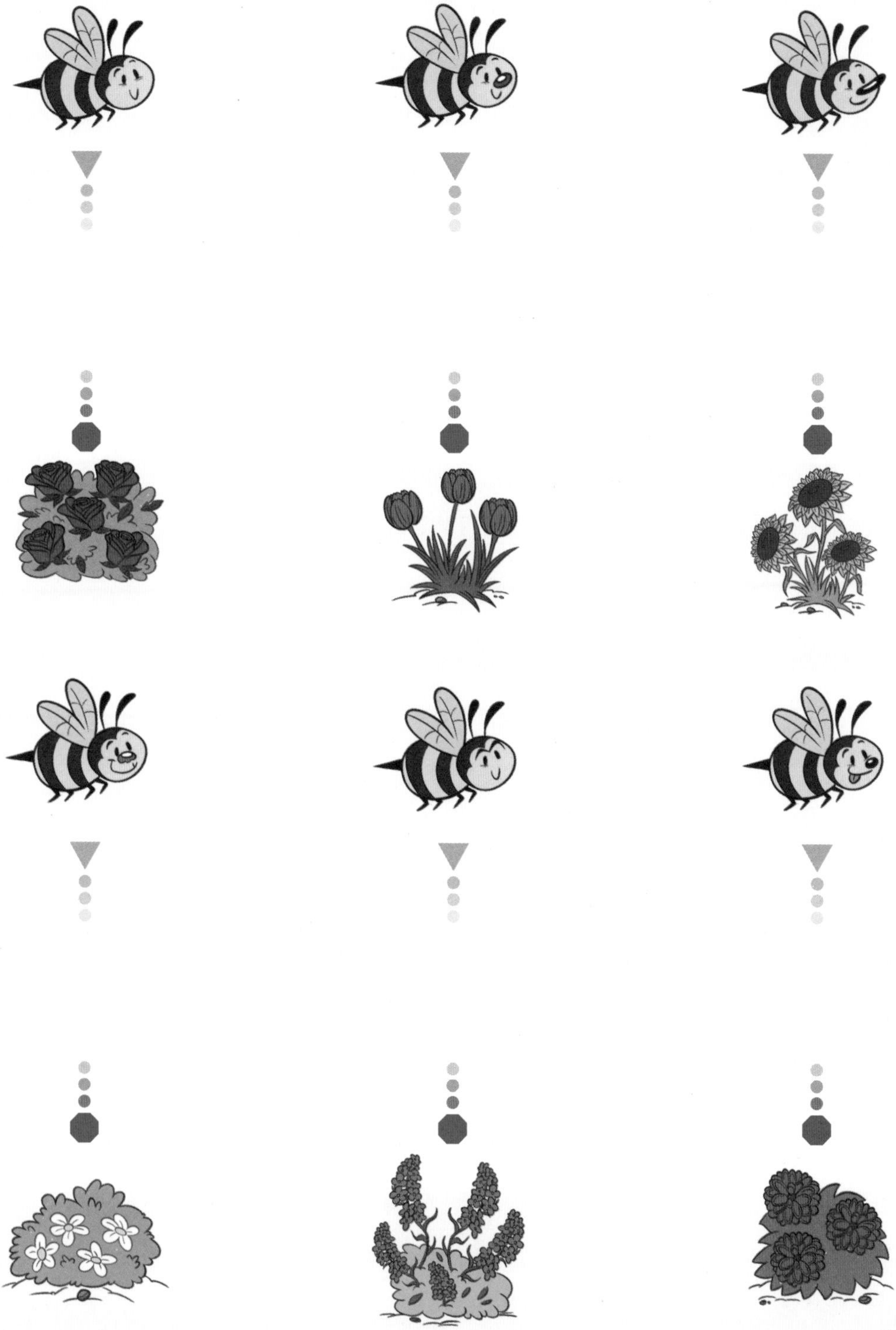

WELL DONE! STICKER

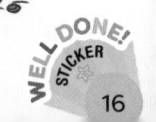

★ HEY, GROWN-UPS! ★
Your child is tracing so many lines! Don't forget
to praise their focus and determination.

Trace the line from each crop to each .

Callie loves tomatoes!
Trace the line from each  to each 🪣.

Trace the line from each MotMot to their favorite seeds.

Enid is feeding the hungry pigs.

Trace the line from each  to each .

Trace the line from each  to each .

Trace the lines from each to each .

23

Trace the line from each 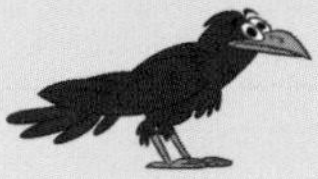 to each 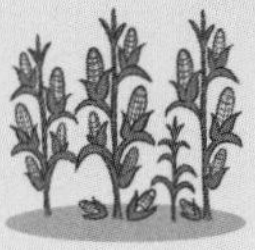.

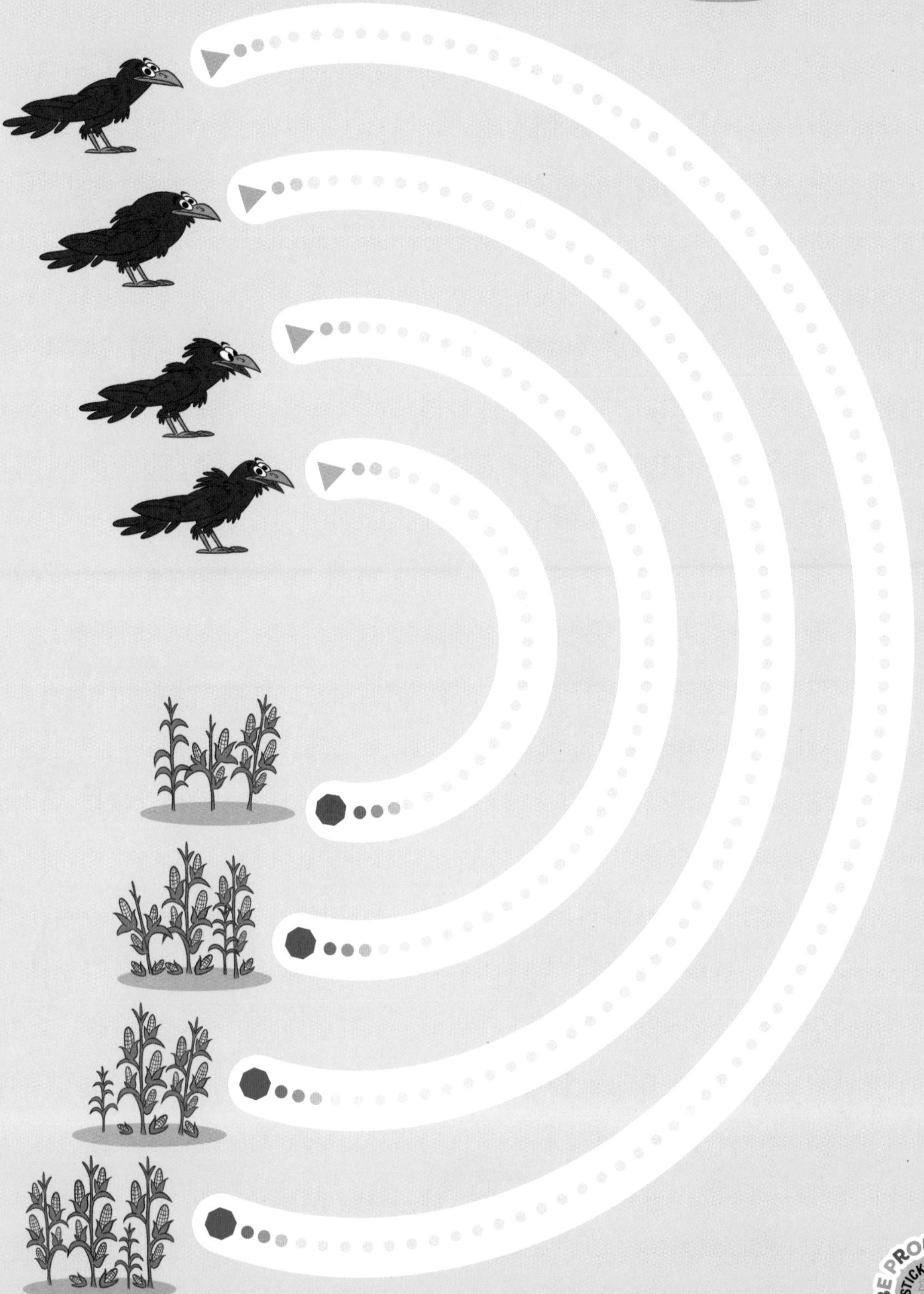

BE PROUD! STICKER

Enid is making crop art!
Trace around the crop circles.

Trace the tire tracks in the field.

Trace the line from each MotMot to their crop.

Trace the line from each MotMot to each 🌿.

Let's TINKER!

Gather these tools and materials.

Bend and roll your materials. Which materials are rigid? Which materials are soft? Which materials do you think can bend and why? Can you bend any of your materials into new shapes?

Some shoeboxes with lids

Tape

String

6 buttons

Glue

Scissors
(with an adult's help)

★ HEY, GROWN-UPS! ★

Ask your child to use their materials to make some shapes on pages 27 and 28. Bend the string along the tracing line or place the buttons along a path. This will reinforce these letter shapes and help your child practice their motor-control skills.

Let's MAKE!

Shoebox Wagon!

1. With the help of an adult, **cut** an arm-length piece of string.

● ● ● ▶

2. **Tape** the ends of the string to the front side of the shoebox to make a handle.

3. **Glue** the buttons along the bottom corners of the box, as shown.

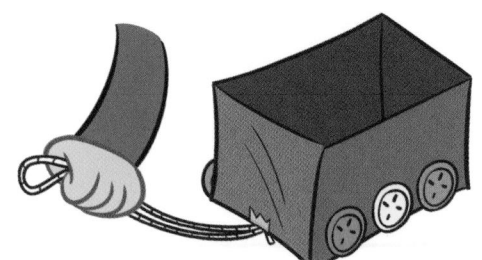

4. **Drag** your wagon around your home! Can it pick up anything along the way?

Let's **ENGINEER** a solution!

Callie and Dimitri are picking strawberries, but their wagon is too small to hold them all! How can they make their wagon hold more strawberries? **Build** a bigger wagon using your materials.

You're a TinkerActive CHAMPION!

Uppercase Letters A–G

Frank is visiting the greenhouse. Draw a line **from A to D** in alphabetical order while saying each letter aloud.

Amelia loves to water the flowers.
Draw a line **from A to D** in alphabetical
order while saying each letter aloud.

A

B

C

D

Enid is picking flowers for her friends. Color by letter. Say each letter name and sound aloud as you color.

A yellow   B orange   C red   D pink

Brian made a tulip arrangement! Color by letter.
Say each letter name and sound aloud as you color.

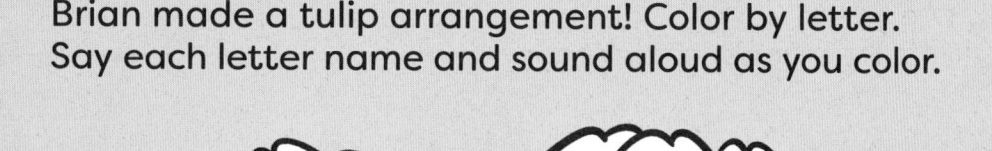

A pink

B red

C blue

D yellow

Trace each letter by following the lines in number order.

Trace each letter by following the lines in number order.

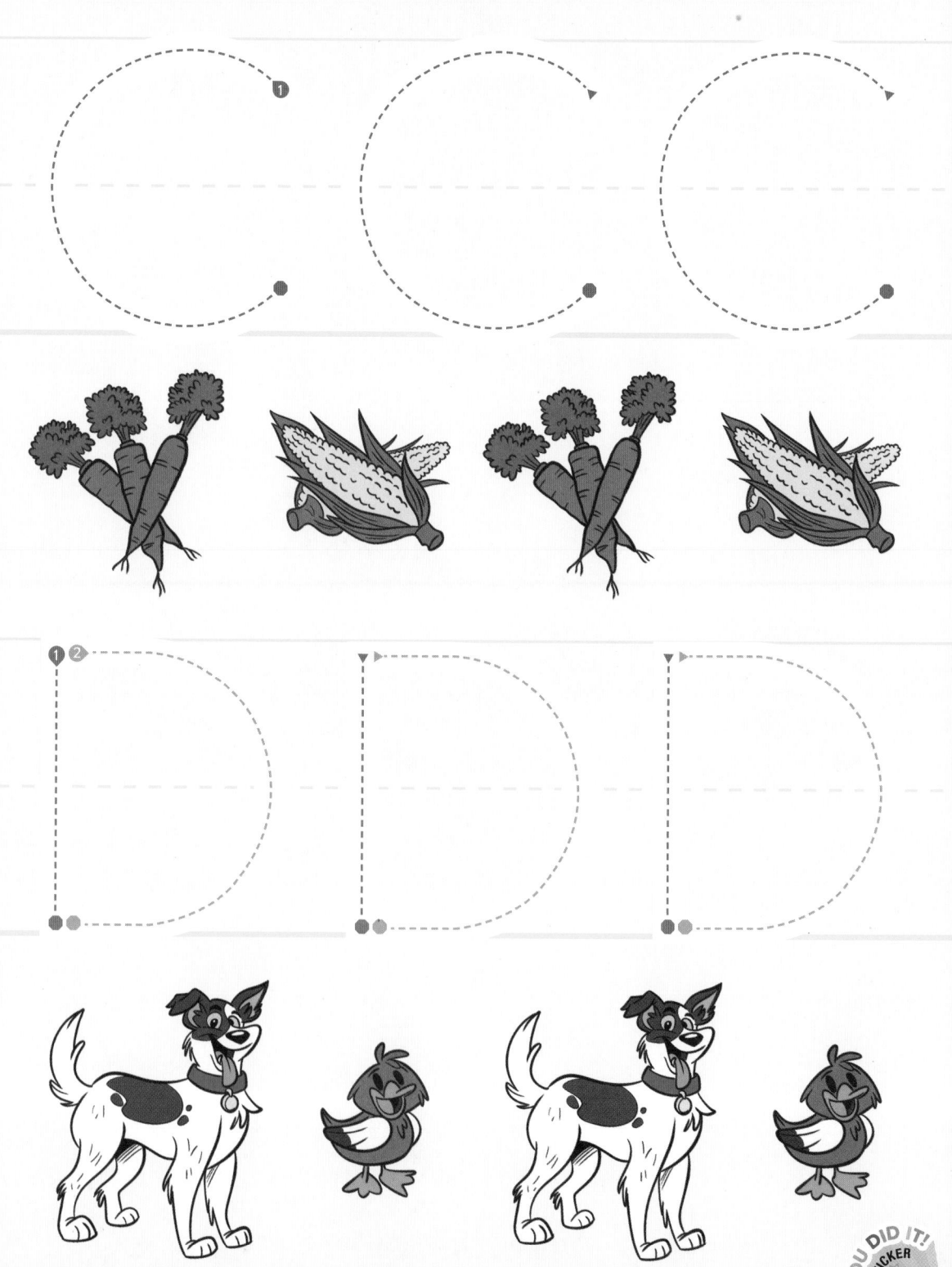

Callie is planting a seed! Draw a line **from A to D** in alphabetical order while saying each letter aloud.

Dimitri spilled the watering can! Draw a line **from A to G** in alphabetical order while saying each letter aloud.

GREAT WORK! STICKER

Draw a line **from A to G** in alphabetical order while saying each letter aloud.

Amelia is arranging seeds in the flower box. Color by letter. Say each letter name and sound aloud as you color.

E brown   F orange   G green

Watch out for the sprinkler, Frank! Color by letter.
Say each letter name and sound aloud as you color.

A gray C light blue E green G yellow
B blue D orange F pink

D
D
D
E
B
G
A
E
E
A
C
F
F
E

Trace each letter by following the lines in number order.

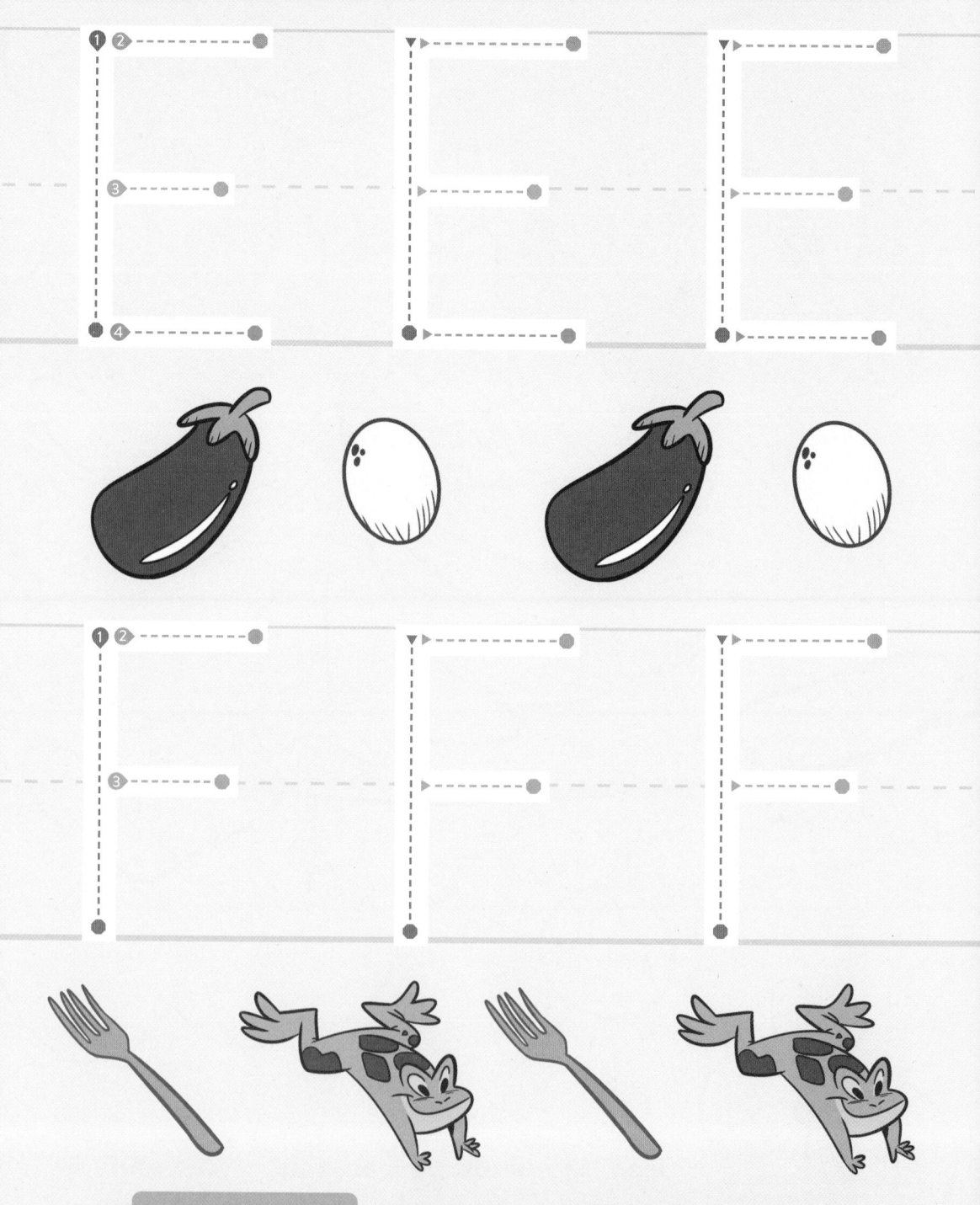

WAY TO GO! STICKER

Trace each letter by following the lines in number order.

Brian is delivering flowers to his friends. Draw a line **from A to G** in alphabetical order while saying each letter aloud.

Gather these tools and materials.

Hold the different materials in your hands. Can you mold, twist, or arrange the materials into the letters A, B, C, D, E, F, or G? Do any of the materials start with a letter you just practiced?

7 craft sticks

Green washable marker

Stickers from page 128

Pipe cleaners

Black or brown modeling clay

Aluminum foil

★ HEY, GROWN-UPS! ★

Use the traceable letters from the previous pages to help your child form letters with their materials. Place the clay or pipe cleaners directly on the page and help your child bend and mold them into a letter.

Flower Patch Match!

1. **Color** the craft sticks green to make flower stems.

2. Use the stickers from page 128 to decorate the tops of the craft sticks.

3. Roll the modeling clay into 7 patches of soil.

4. Place one craft stick into each clay patch of soil.

5. Arrange your craft flowers in alphabetical order.

★ HEY, GROWN-UPS! ★

You can find all the stickers at the end of this book. Peeling stickers is great practice for improving fine motor control. If your child has difficulty at first, peel one corner and ask them to remove the sticker the rest of the way. Your child will gradually develop the skills to peel and place stickers on their own!

Let's ENGINEER a solution!

It's winter in Tinker Town, and Enid and Frank want to protect their flowers from the cold. How can you keep the flowers warm? **Use** your materials to build a shelter for your flowers.

You're a TinkerActive CHAMPION!

Amelia and Dimitri are racing horses to the stables. Draw a line **from A to K** in alphabetical order while saying each letter aloud.

Callie is riding her horse, Jumper. Draw a line **from A to K** in alphabetical order while saying each letter aloud.

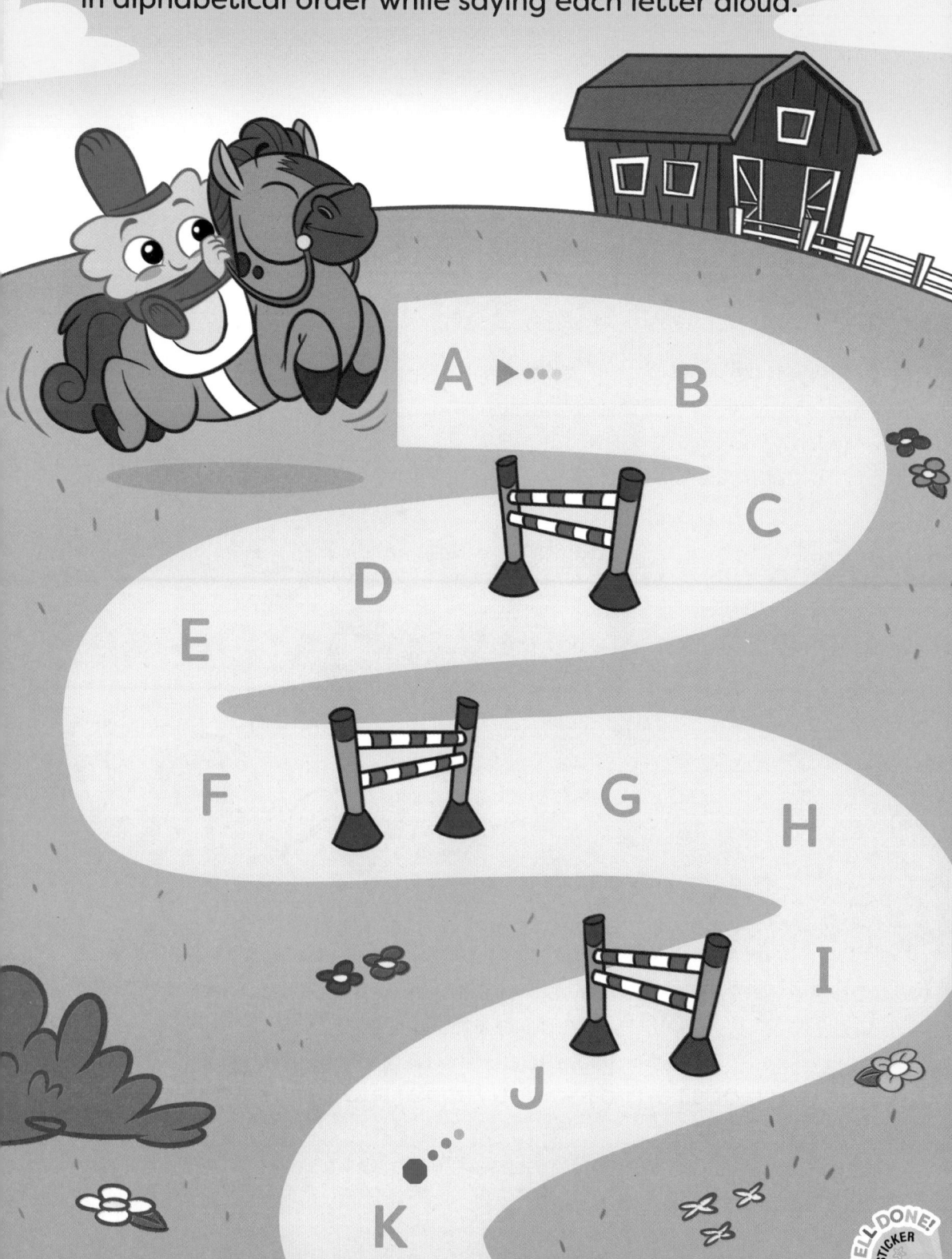

Color by letter. Say each letter name and sound aloud as you color.

H yellow   **I** green   **J** blue   **K** purple

★ HEY, GROWN-UPS! ★

Instead of repeating "Good job," try showing your admiration for different parts of their work. For example, praise your child with "Wow! I love the colors you're using for the saddles." This shows that you're paying close attention to their work and exposes them to different vocabulary.

Amelia's horse won the race! Color by letter. Say each letter name and sound aloud as you color.

H yellow	**L** green
I orange	**M** blue
J red	**N** gray
K brown	

Trace each letter by following the lines in number order.

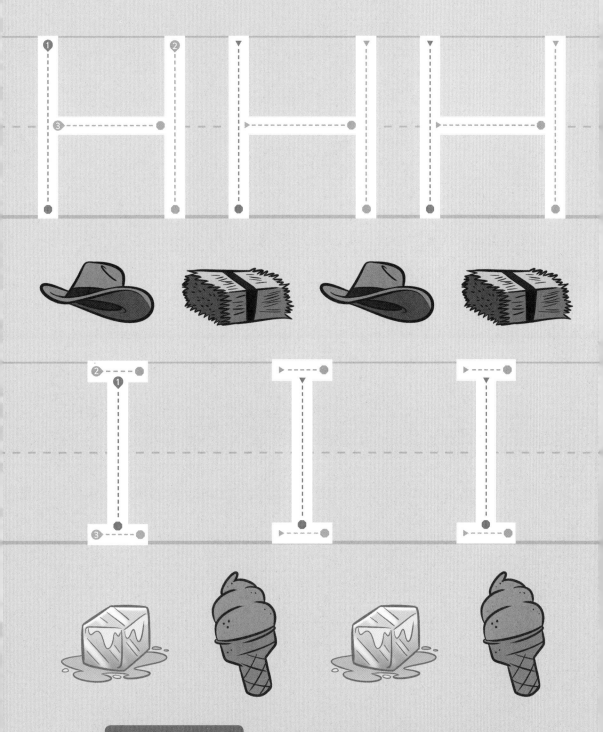

★ HEY, GROWN-UPS! ★

Ask your child to tell you words that start with each letter. Connecting letter names to letter sounds is a big step toward reading!

51

Trace each letter by following the lines in number order.

Dimitri needs the saddle for his horse.
Draw a line **from A to K** in alphabetical
order while saying each letter aloud.

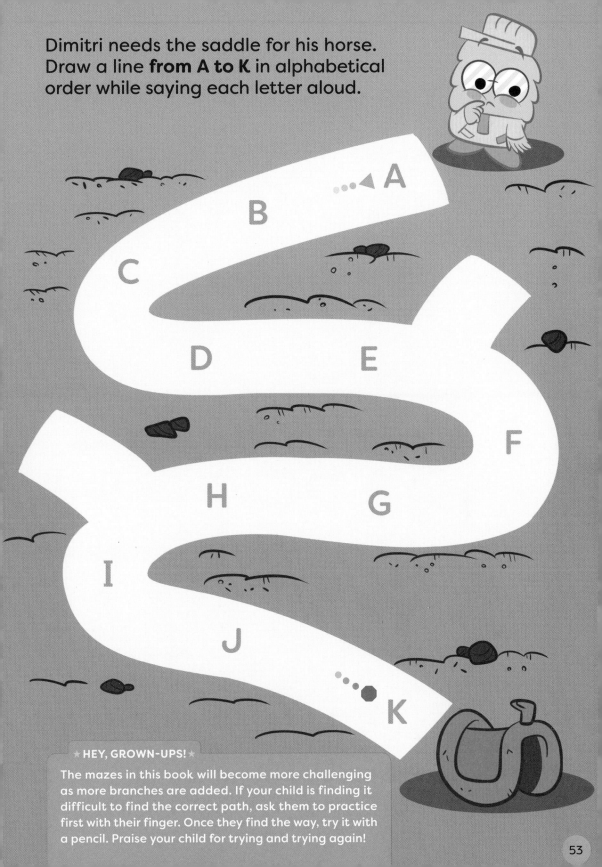

A

B

C

D E

F

H G

I

J

K

Callie is taking Jumper to her stall.
Draw a line **from A to N** in alphabetical
order while saying each letter aloud.

Frank is brushing his horse. Draw a line **from A to N** in alphabetical order while saying each letter aloud.

56

Color by letter. Say each letter name and sound aloud as you color.

| L | yellow | M | orange | N | brown |

Amelia won a race! Color by letter.
Say each letter name and sound
aloud as you color.

| **H** yellow | **I** red | **J** green |
| **K** orange | **L** pink | **M** blue | **N** purple |

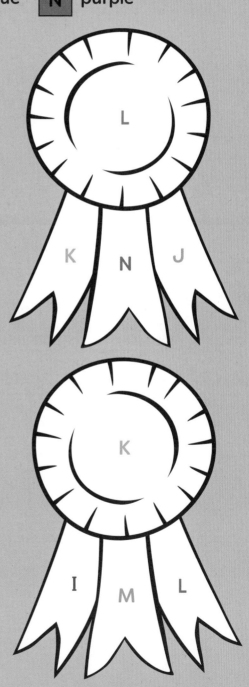

Trace the letters by following the lines in number order.

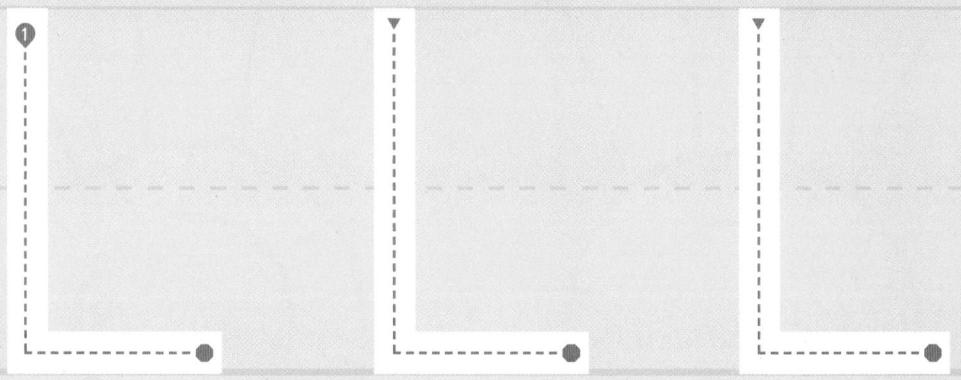

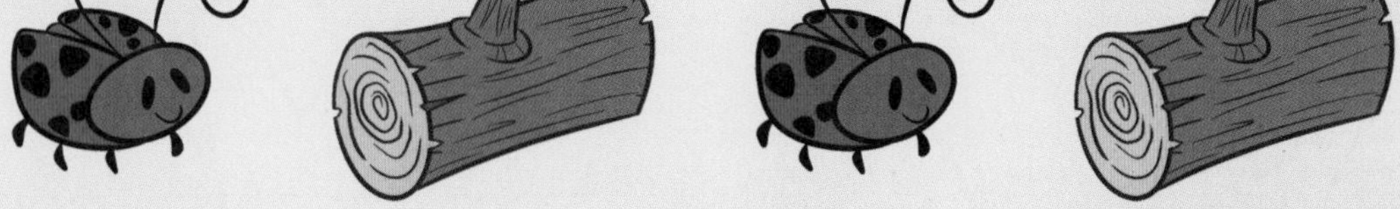

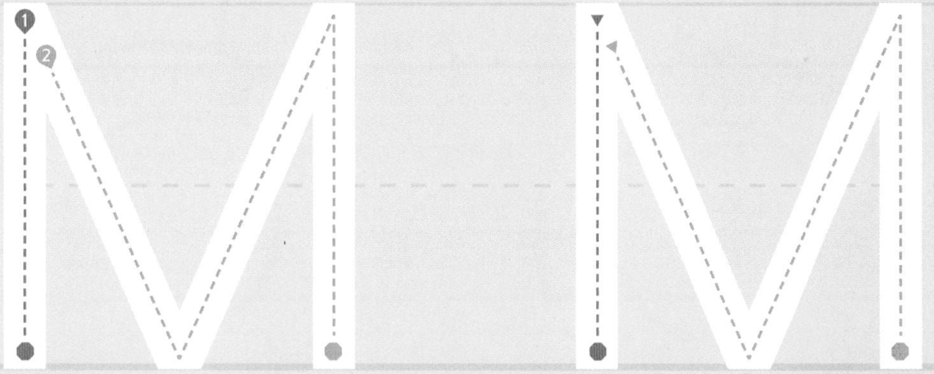

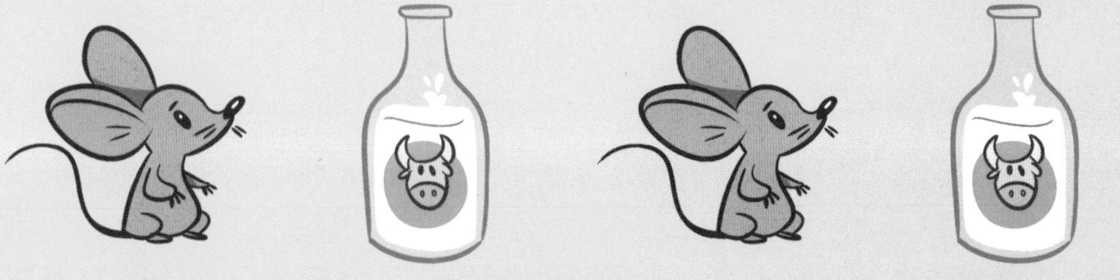

L L L

M M M

Trace the letters by following the lines in number order.

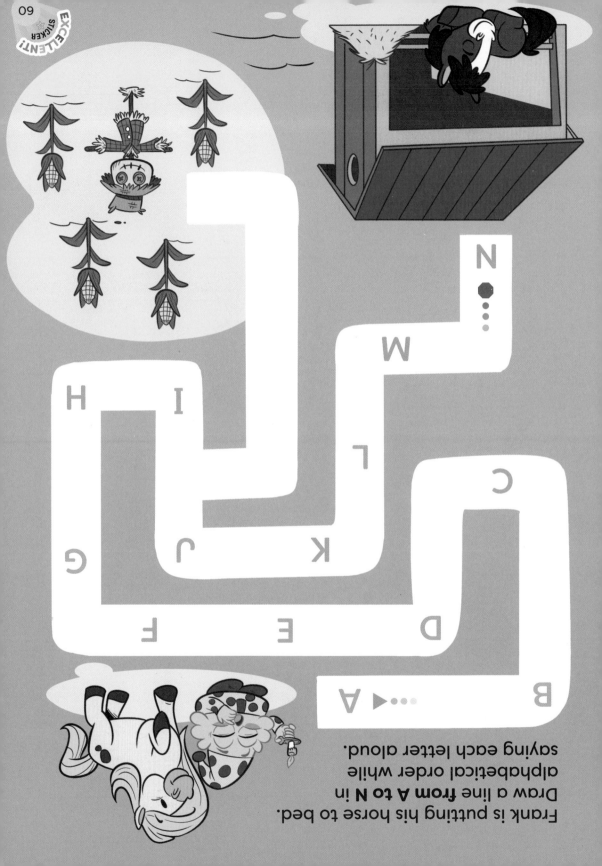

Frank is putting his horse to bed.
Draw a line **from A to N** in
alphabetical order while
saying each letter aloud.

Let's TINKER!

Gather these tools and materials.

Play with, touch, and roll your materials. **Find** the materials that start with the letters you've learned so far. Can you make those letter shapes with your materials?

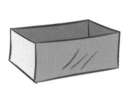
Shoebox
(without lid)

Gift-wrap tube

Tape

Craft sticks

Stickers from page 128

Washable markers

Construction paper

Let's MAKE!

Cardboard Racing Horse!

1. **Tape** the gift-wrap tube inside the shoebox in the middle, as shown.

2. **Place** the eyes, ears, nose, and mane stickers from page 128 on the front of the shoebox to make your horse's face.

3. **Decorate** your horse with washable markers.

4. **Go** for a ride! Can you jump over any obstacles?

Let's **ENGINEER** a solution!

Brian and Amelia keep bringing their horses, Leaper, Millie, and Nelly, to the wrong stalls! How can they make sure each horse gets to the right place? **Use** your materials to make a sign for each horse that shows where each horse lives.

You're a TinkerActive CHAMPION!

► LET'S LEARN ABOUT

Uppercase Letters O–U

It's apple-picking season! Draw a line **from A to R** in alphabetical order while saying each letter aloud.

★ **HEY, GROWN-UPS!** ★

Encourage your child through these challenging mazes with phrases like "Keep going!" or "I'm proud of the way you are learning your letters!" The goal is for them to become familiar with the letters' shapes and sounds.

63

Frank's favorite apples are Red Delicious. Draw a line **from A to R** in alphabetical order while saying each letter aloud.

WELL DONE! STICKER

Amelia loves eating apples. Color by letter. Say each letter name and sound aloud as you color.

O yellow   Q green

P light green   R red

Dimitri picked his favorite apples!
Color by letter. Say each letter name
and sound aloud as you color.

M	yellow	P	blue
N	red	Q	light green
O	green	R	gray

GOOD JOB! STICKER

Trace each letter by following the lines in number order.

Trace each letter by following the lines in number order.

Q Q

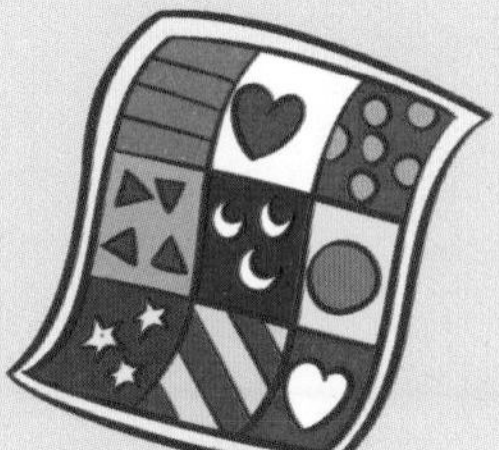
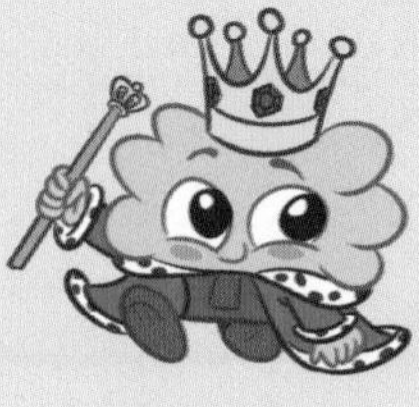
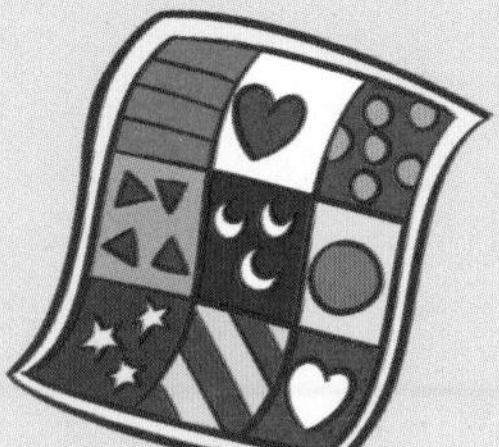
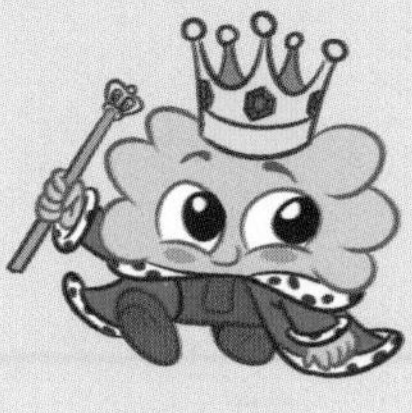

R R R

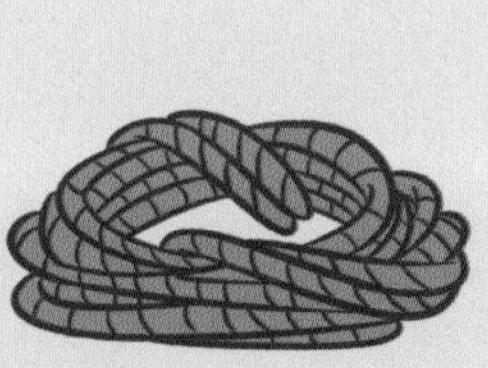
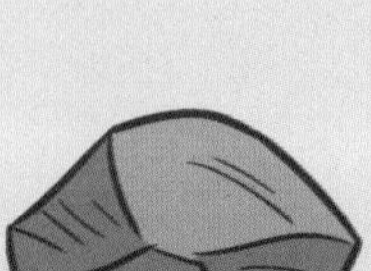
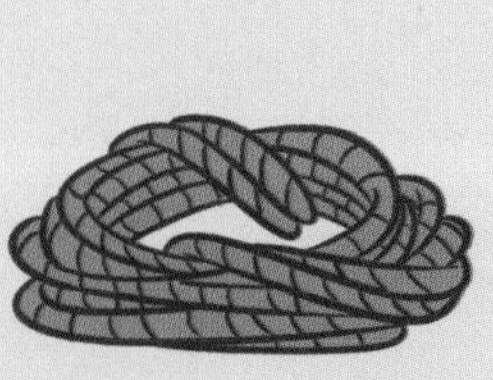
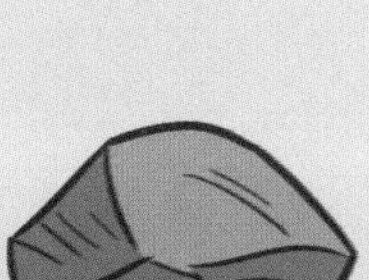

YOU DID IT! STICKER

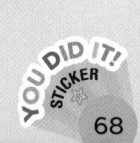

Callie baked an apple pie for the picnic!
Draw a line **from A to R** in alphabetical
order while saying each letter aloud.

A
K   L
D   C   B   J   M
E   I   N
F   G   H
R   Q   P   O

Draw a line **from A to U** in alphabetical order while saying each letter aloud.

Draw a line **from A to U** in alphabetical order while saying each letter aloud.

★ HEY, GROWN-UPS! ★

As your child learns more and more of the alphabet, the connecting dots will continue to get longer. It is okay if your child's pencil strays from the path or if they must pick up their pencil from the page and put it down again—these are long and complex lines for their little hands!

Color by letter. Say each letter name and sound aloud as you color.

S green T yellow U red

Brian is swinging from the apple tree! Color by letter.
Say each letter name **and** sound aloud as you color.

P pink   **R** red   **T** green

Q yellow   **S** brown   **U** orange

Trace each letter by following the lines in number order.

S S S

T T T

Trace each letter by following the lines in number order.

★ HEY, GROWN-UPS! ★

Full-body movements can help your child practice writing with straight and curved lines. If your child is having difficulty writing these letters, have them draw the lines in the air with a finger. You can also create extra practice on the write-and-wipe game board by drawing dotted lines that your child can trace.

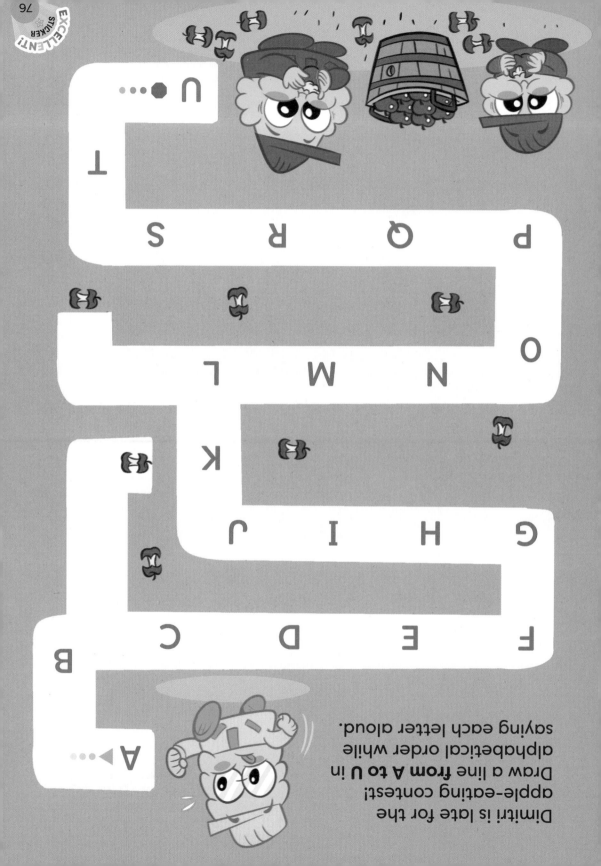

EXCELLENT! STICKER

Dimitri is late for the apple-eating contest! Draw a line **from A to U** in alphabetical order while saying each letter aloud.

A ●●●▶

B

C D E F

G H I J

K

L M N O

P Q R S

T

U ●●●■

Let's TINKER!

Gather these tools and materials.

Squish and push your materials. Can you draw letters with any of your materials? **Make** letters with your other materials that match what you've drawn.

Construction paper
(at least blue and brown)

Cupcake liners
(at least 4)

Washable markers
(at least green and red)

Cotton balls

Glue

Aluminum foil

★ HEY, GROWN-UPS! ★

Old-fashioned glue bottles are great for little hands (even if they are a tad messier!). The motion of squeezing out glue, ketchup, or toothpaste strengthens the whole hand, which makes gripping a pencil and early writing easier. Once the glue bottle is empty, fill it up with water for more squeezing practice.

Let's MAKE!   Paper Apple Tree!

1. Tear out a tree trunk shape from the brown construction paper.

2. Glue the tree trunk to the bottom edge of the blue construction paper.

●●● ▶

3. **Color** the cupcake liners with a green marker.

5. **Color** a handful of cotton balls with a red marker.

4. **Glue** the cupcake liners to the top of the trunk to form the top of the tree.

6. **Glue** the cotton ball apples to your tree. Can you glue your apples to make a letter from O to U?

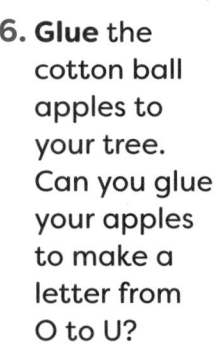

Let's **ENGINEER** a solution!

Brian and Frank went apple picking, but they forgot their basket! How can they carry their pickings? **Color** some more cotton ball apples and build something to carry them with. What materials are strong enough to carry cotton ball apples?

You're a TinkerActive CHAMPION!

Amelia wants to meet her friends at the end of the corn maze! Draw a line **from A to X** while saying each letter aloud.

A · · · B C D

H G F E

I

J

K L M N O P

Q

R

V U T S

W · · · X

Enid can't wait to chow down on corn! Draw a line from **A to X** in alphabetical order while saying each letter aloud.

Color by letter.
Say each letter
name and sound
aloud as you
color.

V	red
W	blue
X	orange

Color by letter. Say each letter name and sound aloud as you color.

T	orange	**V**	pink	**X**	yellow
S	purple	**U**	red	**W**	green

Trace each letter by following the lines in number order.

★ HEY, GROWN-UPS! ★

For extra practice writing Vs and Ws, ask your child to draw zigzag patterns on the write-and-wipe game board.

83

Trace each letter by following the lines in number order.

① ② X X X

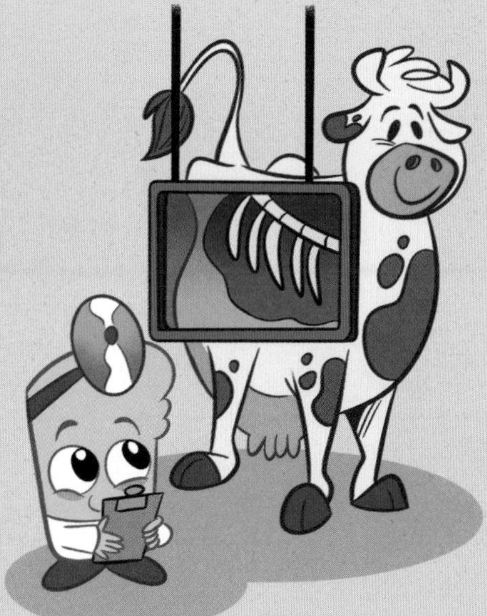

V W X

Dimitri's favorite corn is the popped kind! Draw a line **from A to X** in alphabetical order while saying each letter aloud.

Callie's pumpkin is the largest in the patch. Draw a line **from A to Z** in alphabetical order while saying each letter aloud.

Amelia carved a jack-o'-lantern!
Draw a line **from A to Z** in alphabetical
order while saying each letter aloud.

Color by letter. Say each letter name
and sound aloud as you color.

Y pink   **Z** yellow

Which MotMot won the pumpkin-carving contest? Color by
letter. Say each letter name and sound aloud as you color.

V orange   W green   X purple

Y blue   Z pink

Trace each letter by following the lines in number order.

Trace the letters. Say each letter aloud as you trace.

A B C D

E F G H I

J K L M

★ HEY, GROWN-UPS! ★

Your child is drawing many letters on this page at a smaller size than before! Encourage your child with phrases like "I'm so proud of the letters you are writing!" or "You're working really hard on your letters!"

W X Y Z

R S T U V

N O P Q

Trace the letters. Say each letter aloud as you trace.

Let's  TINKER!

Gather these tools and materials.

What do your materials do? Can they do more than one thing? **Stack** or put them together to make the letters A through Z.

4 paper plates

Orange washable paint

Paint brush

Washable markers

Large beans or buttons

Glue stick

★ HEY, GROWN-UPS! ★

If your little learner enjoys messy, tactile activities, encourage them to dip a finger into the washable paint. Then have them draw letters on paper or poster board.

Let's MAKE!

Pumpkin Tambourines!

1. **Paint** one side of each paper plate orange and let dry.

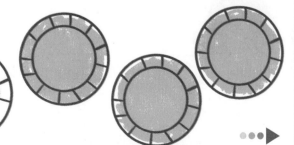

2. **Draw** pumpkin leaves and stems on the orange side of each plate.

3. **Lay** 2 plates colored side down, and pour the beans or buttons into the middle of each plate.

4. **Add** glue to the edges of the filled plates. Then **place** your remaining painted plates on top, colored side out. **Let** dry.

5. **Shake**, shake, shake your pumpkin tambourine! **Have** a pumpkin party with a friend or family member!

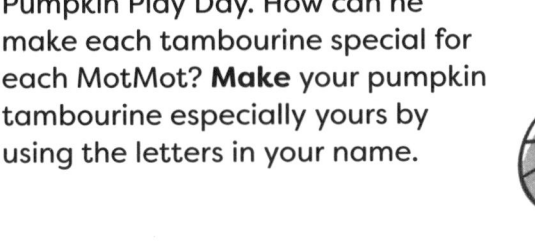

Let's ENGINEER a solution!

Dimitri is making pumpkin tambourines for the MotMots for Pumpkin Play Day. How can he make each tambourine special for each MotMot? **Make** your pumpkin tambourine especially yours by using the letters in your name.

Enid is exploring the farmer's market. Say the name of each animal or object aloud. Then trace the first letter of each word.

Ant

Bee

Dog

Can

Egg

Say each letter sound aloud. Then color the picture that begins with the same letter sound.

B

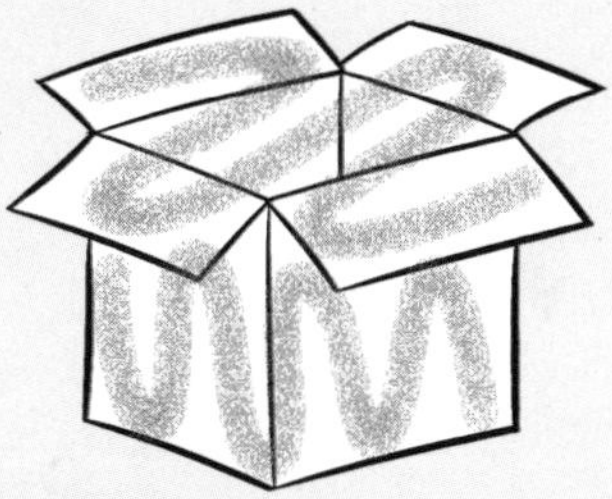

D

E

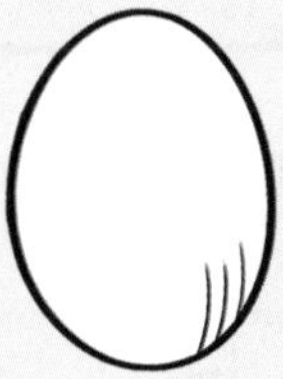

A

C

96

Name each picture aloud. Then circle the letter that matches the first letter sound.

Ax   F   Ⓐ

Book   B   G

Cow   C   B

Duck   A   D

Egg   C   E

Name each picture aloud. Then circle the letter that matches the first letter sound.

Elephant — A E

Dog — E D

Corn — C A

Bat — C B

Apple — A D

Say the name of each animal or object aloud. Then trace the first letter of each word.

Fox

Goat

Hat

Ice

★ HEY, GROWN-UPS! ★

After your child finishes tracing each letter, ask them to tell you other words that start with that letter. Share your excitement when they say a word that matches the beginning letter!

Say each letter sound aloud. Then color the picture that begins with the same letter sound.

Name each picture aloud. Then circle the letter that matches the first letter sound.

 Grapes G B

 Ink D I

 Fish F A

 Horse H C

★ HEY, GROWN-UPS! ★

Make an interactive scavenger hunt with beginning letter sounds! Say a letter sound aloud. Then hunt together around your home for an object that starts with the same letter sound. When your child finds one, ask them to draw the letter on the write-and-wipe game board.

Name each picture aloud. Then circle the letter that matches the first letter sound.

Fan

Goose

B A F

G D E

Hen

Ice cream

F H I

I B C

Amelia and Brian are shopping at the market. Say the name of each object aloud. Then trace the first letter of each word.

Jam

Leaf

Key

Milk

★ HEY, GROWN-UPS! ★

Your child is still learning how to draw letters within the handwriting guidelines. It's okay if they write outside the lines. Using an eraser to correct mistakes also builds muscles and motor-control skills!

Say each letter sound aloud. Then color the picture that
begins with the same letter sound.

Name each picture aloud. Then circle the letter that matches the first letter sound.

Lamp   M   L

Map   D   M

Jar   J   G

Kite   E   K

★ HEY, GROWN-UPS! ★

Practice this activity at home! Grab some sticky notes and some small items that start with J, K, L, and M, like juice boxes, lemons, keys, and mittens. Label each sticky note with one letter. Ask your child to organize the items under the sticky notes with the matching beginning letter sounds.

Name each picture aloud. Then circle the letter that matches the first letter sound.

Juice

A H J

Key

K M D

Log

B L C

Mug

M F E

With the help of an adult, cut out the letters at the bottom of the page. Name each picture aloud and place the first letter of the word next to the picture.

A B C D E F G

H I J K L M

With the help of an adult, cut out the letters at the top of the page. Name each picture aloud and place the first letter of the word next to the picture.

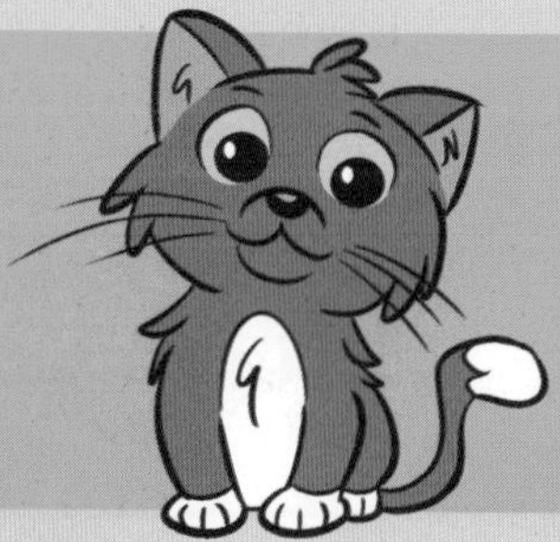

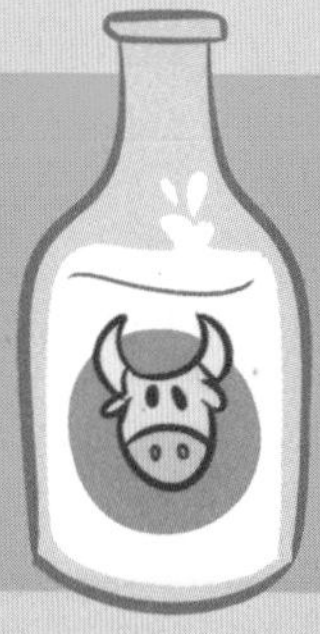

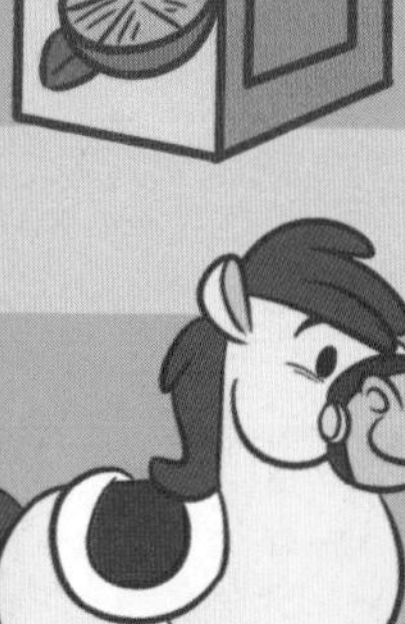

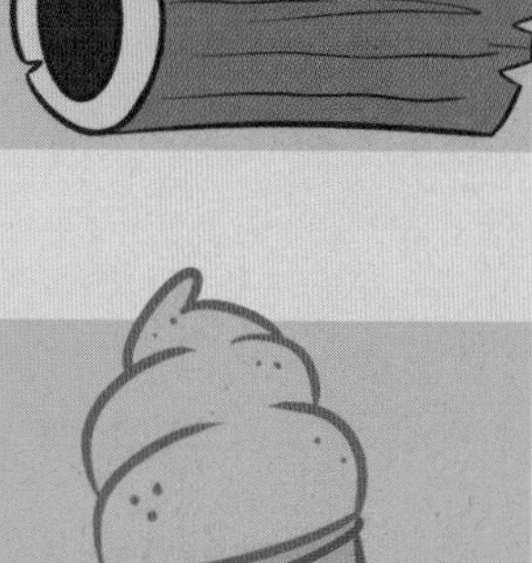

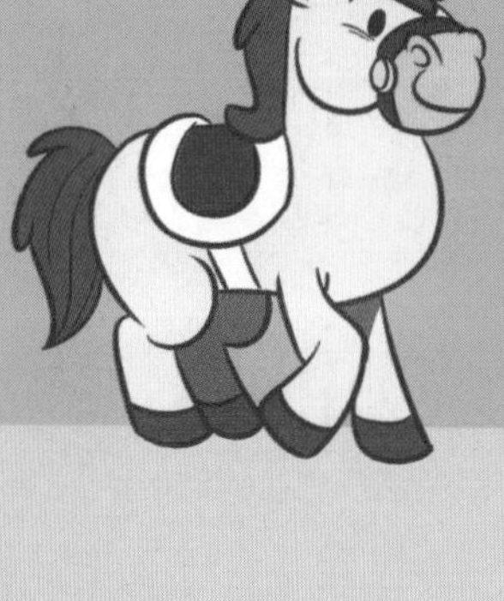

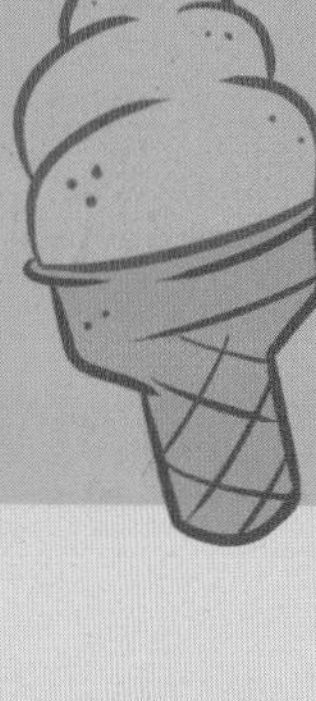

EXCELLENT! STICKER

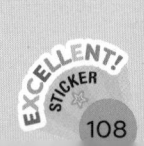

Let's TINKER!

Stretch, move, and roll your materials. Now **say** each object name aloud. Which letter matches each first letter sound? Can you make those first letters with your materials?

Balloons
(at least 7)

Washable marker

Painter's tape

Broom

Pillows

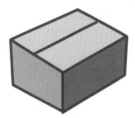

Cardboard boxes

Let's MAKE!

Cowabunga Herd!

1. With the help of an adult, **inflate** 7 or more balloons.

2. With the help of an adult, **write** one letter (A, B, C, D, E, F, or G) on each balloon.

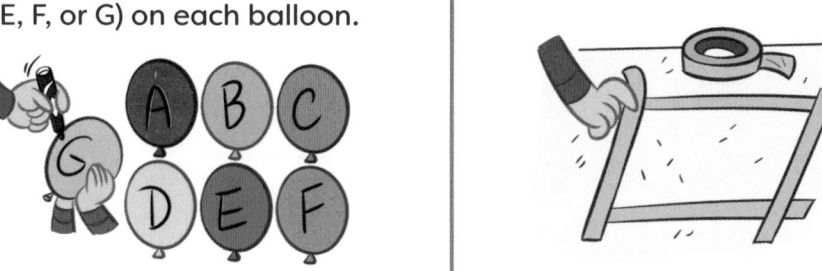

3. Create a large cow pen on the floor with painter's tape.

4. Push your balloon cows into the pen with your broom! When the balloon is in the pen, **say** the letter on the balloon aloud!

★ **HEY, GROWN-UPS!** ★

Balloons can be lots of fun, especially when they pop! But for children who may be sensitive to loud auditory stimuli, substitute small beach balls or tennis balls for the balloons.

Let's **ENGINEER** a solution!

Callie's cows keep escaping their pen and wandering into the farmer's market! The fence around the pen just isn't tall enough! How can Callie make her pen taller? **Use** your materials to build a tall pen for your cow balloons.

You're a TinkerActive CHAMPION!

Amelia is visiting the farm's petting zoo! Say the name of each animal or object aloud. Then trace the first letter of each word.

 Nest

 Orange

 Pig  Quilt

 Rabbit

Say each letter sound aloud. Then color the picture that begins with the same letter sound.

N

O

P

Q

R

Name each picture aloud. Then circle the letter that matches the first letter sound.

Pup   C   P

Ox   O   G

Rat   R   E

Quilt   B   Q

Nest   N   O

Name each picture aloud. Then circle the letter that matches the first letter sound.

Net

M N E

Pig

G D P

Rug

R C A

Owl

O H K

Enid and Brian are petting the sheep! Say the name of each animal or object aloud. Then trace the first letter of each word.

 Sun

Turtle

 Umbrella

Vegetables

Say each letter sound aloud. Then color the picture that begins with the same letter sound.

S

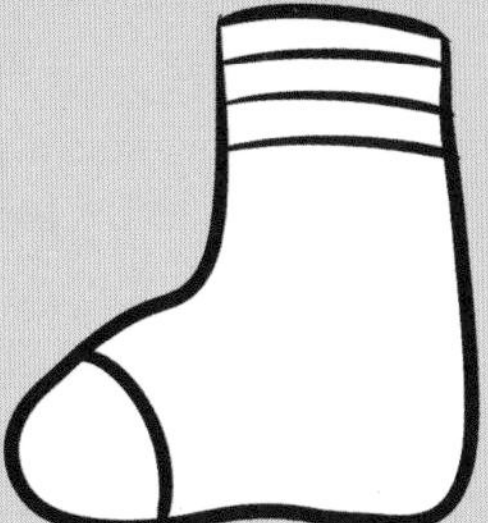

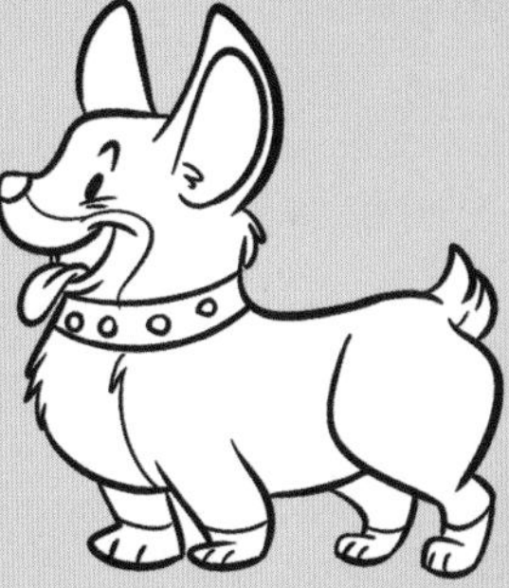

T

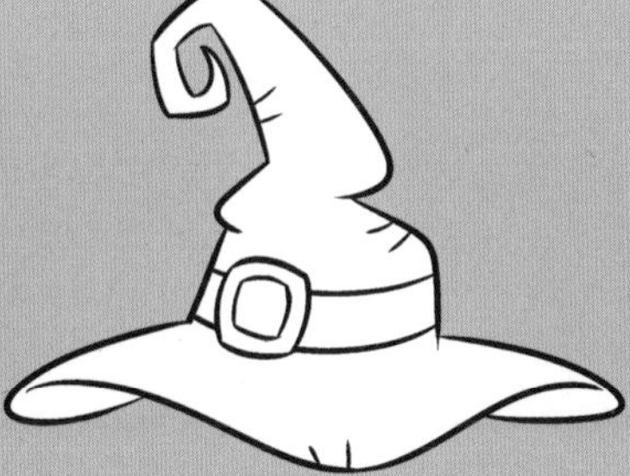

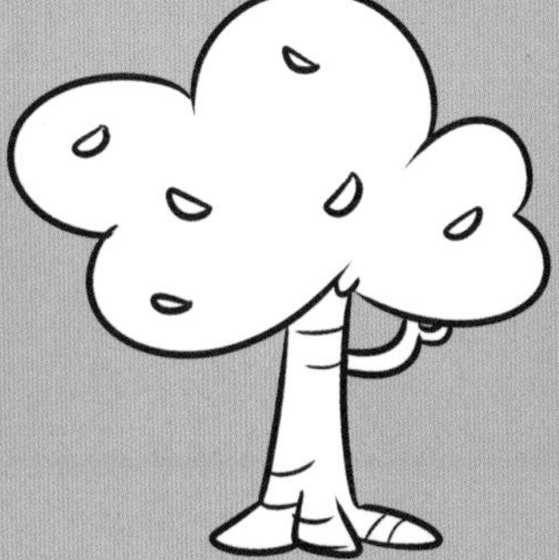

U

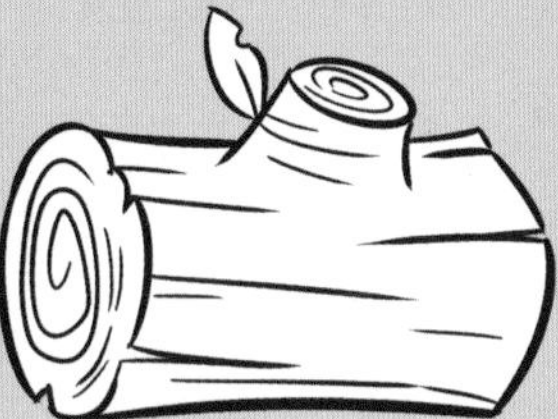

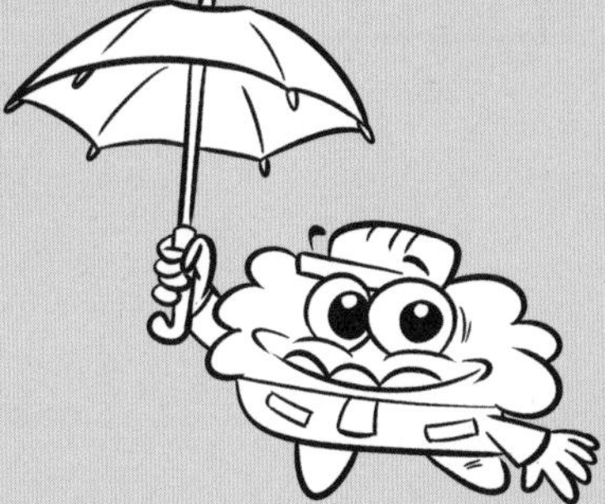

V

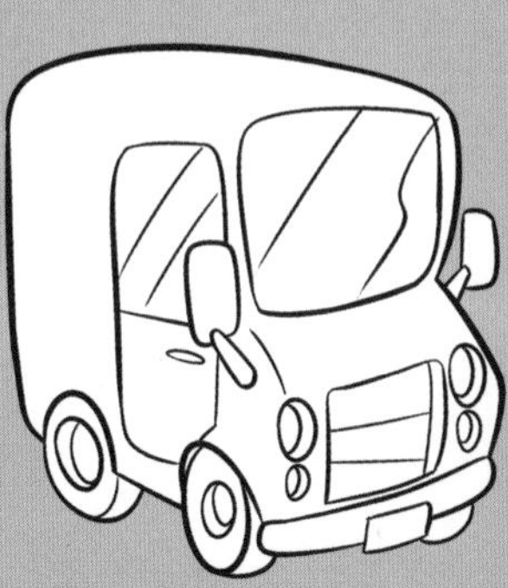

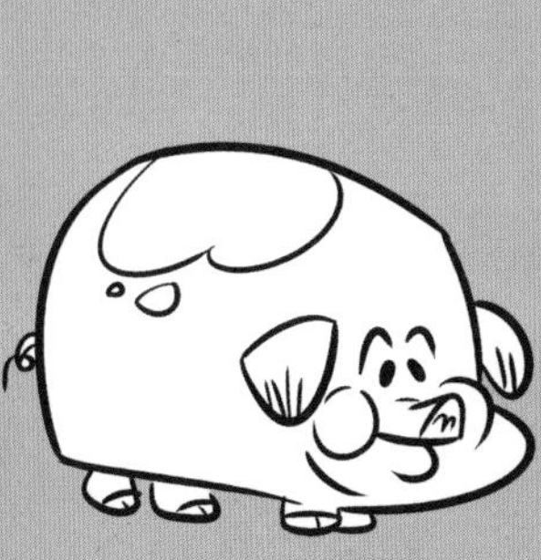

YOU DID IT! STICKER

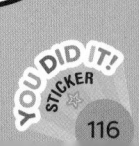

Name each picture aloud. Then circle the letter that matches the first letter sound.

 Seed   S   R

 Tomato   T   G

 Umbrella   K   U

Veterinarian   C   V

★ HEY, GROWN-UPS! ★

The words on this page are quite large for your little learner. If your child is unfamiliar with the word, say it aloud. Your child will be able to hear the beginning letter sound, even if they are unsure of the other letters.

Name each picture aloud. Then circle the letter that matches the first letter sound.

Ukulele

S P U

Turtle

R B T

Van

A V D

Star

S K M

Amelia and Dimitri are playing veterinarians.
Say the name of each picture aloud.
Then trace the first letter of each word.

Web

X-ray

Yak

Zoo

Say each letter sound aloud. Then color the picture that begins with the same letter sound.

W

X

Y

Z

Name each picture aloud. Then circle the letter that matches the first letter sound.

X-ray

X   S

Zipper

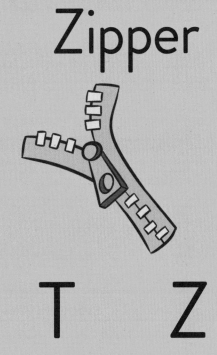

T   Z

Worm

U   W

Yo-yo

Y   H

Y M W

Wagon

B X S

X-ray

D W Y

Yarn

C S Z

Zebra

Name each picture aloud. Then circle the letter that matches the first letter sound.

With the help of an adult, cut out the letters at the bottom of the page. Name each picture aloud and place the first letter of the word next to the picture.

★ HEY, GROWN-UPS! ★

Your child is close to completing this workbook—congratulations! Look back at some of their earlier work and notice the large strides they have made. Let your child know how proud you are of them with phrases like "You worked really hard in this book and it shows!" or "Look how much you've learned!"

N O P Q R S T

U V W X Y Z

With the help of an adult, cut out the letters at the top of the page. Name each picture aloud and place the first letter of the word next to the picture.

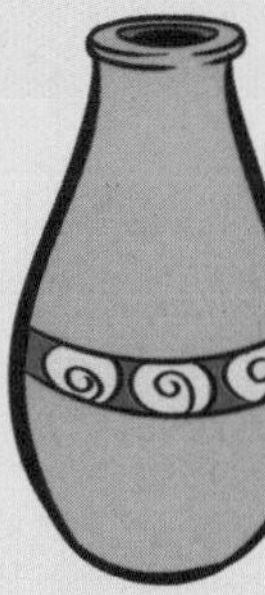

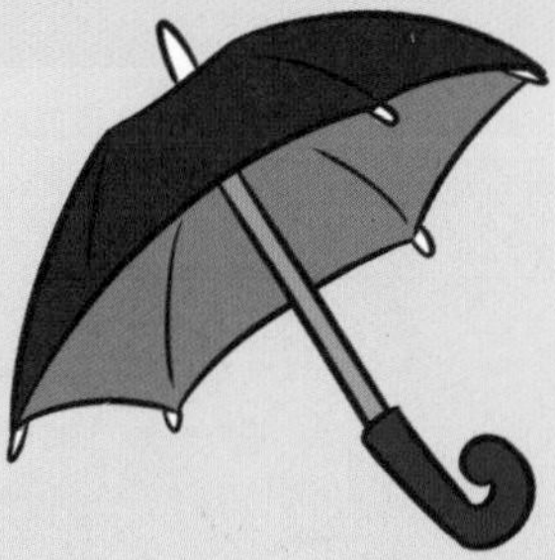

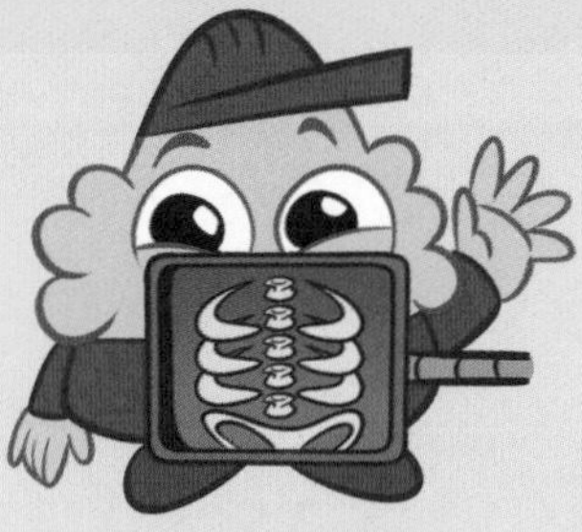

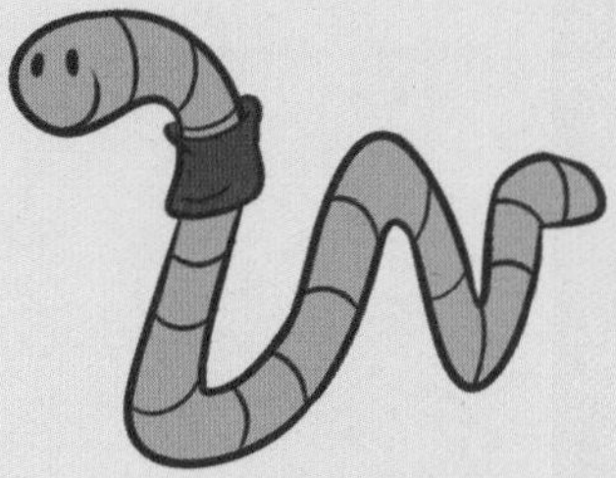

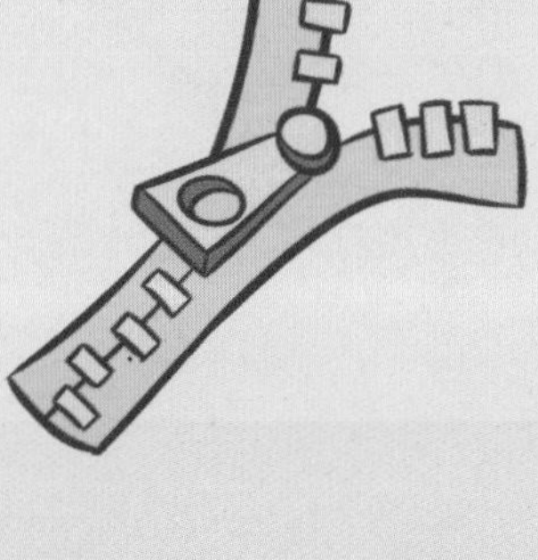

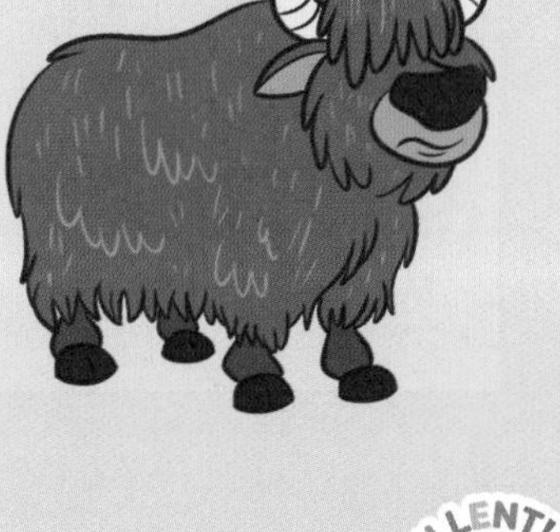

EXCELLENT! STICKER

Let's TINKER!

Gather these tools and materials.

Say the name of each material aloud. Do you know what letters they start with? Can you arrange your materials in alphabetical order? What other letter sounds do you hear in the words?

Construction paper

Scissors
(with an adult's help)

Tape

Stickers from page 129

Cardboard pieces of various sizes

Toy blocks

Let's MAKE!

Petting Zoo Puppets!

1. With the help of an adult, **cut** 8 finger-length strips of construction paper in different colors.

●●●▶

2. Curl each piece of paper around your finger and tape each piece closed.

3. On top of each piece of paper, **place** an animal sticker from page 129.

4. Can you name each animal aloud? **Use** your petting zoo puppets to make a story!

Let's **ENGINEER** a solution!

The petting zoo animals want to play! How can the MotMots make them a playground? **Use** your materials to build obstacles and play sets for your petting zoo puppets.

You're a TinkerActive CHAMPION!

Page 45:

Page 61: